HOME Sweet Home

A HAND-CRAFTED COLORING BOOK

Illustrations by Steve Duffendack

Published in 2015 by:
Spirit Marketing, LLC
315 Westport Rd, Suite 200, Kansas City, MO 64111

hellospiritmarketing.com
© 2015 Spirit Marketing

ISBN: 978-0-9965998-1-8

Designed in Kansas City by Chris Evans, Steve Duffendack, Chris Simmons, and Patrick Sullivan.

For information about custom editions, special sales, and premium and corporate purchases, please contact Spirit Marketing at info@hellospiritmail.com or 1.888.288.3972.

Third Printing, 12/15 in USA

This book belongs to:

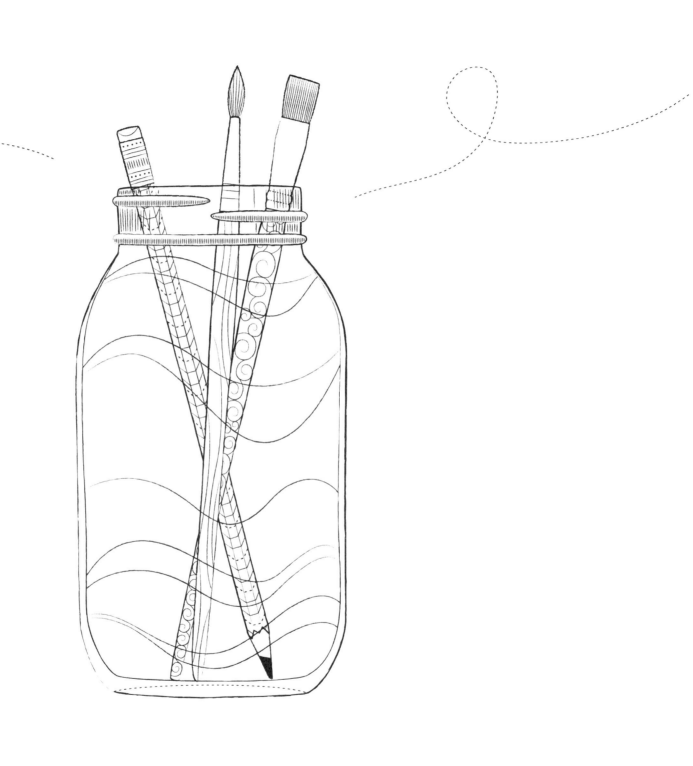

Steve Duffendack

The inspiration and beauty of Steve's surroundings influence his playful creativity each and every day. A lover of all things displaying vibrant color and a good story, Steve was determined by the young age of 10 to become an artist.

Born and raised in Kansas City, Steve works as a freelance illustrator and continues to explore his creativeness through various outlets. He holds a BFA in graphic design with an emphasis in illustration from the University of Missouri and is thankful for his greatest inspirations: Alise, his wife, and their children, Spencer and Annalisa.

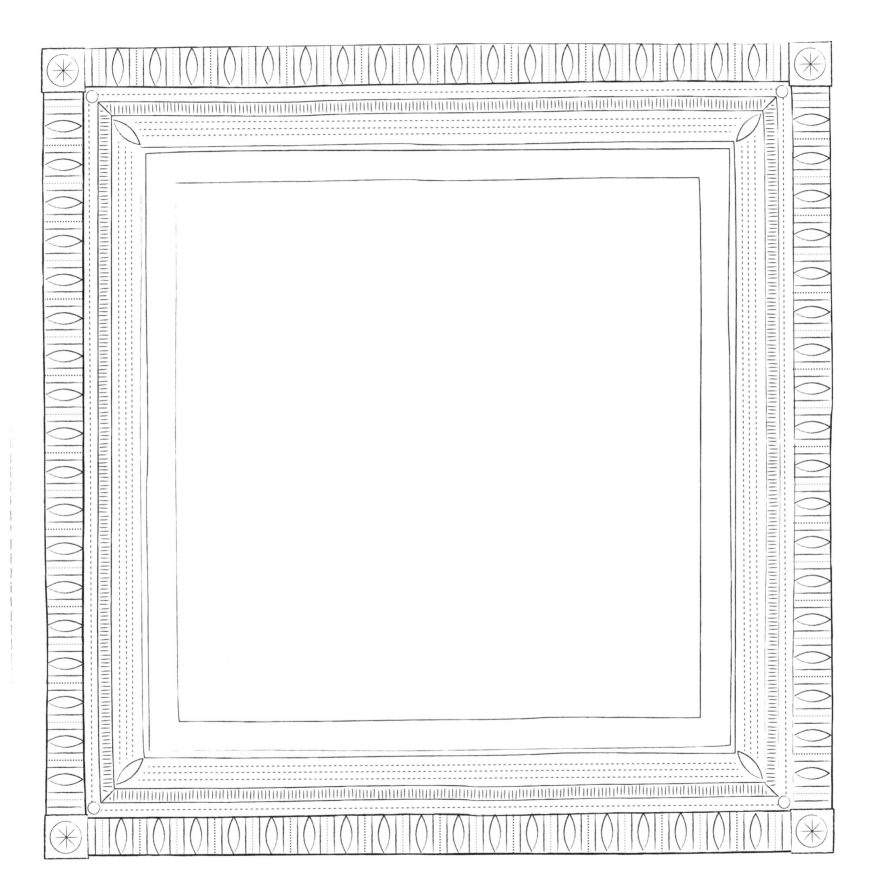

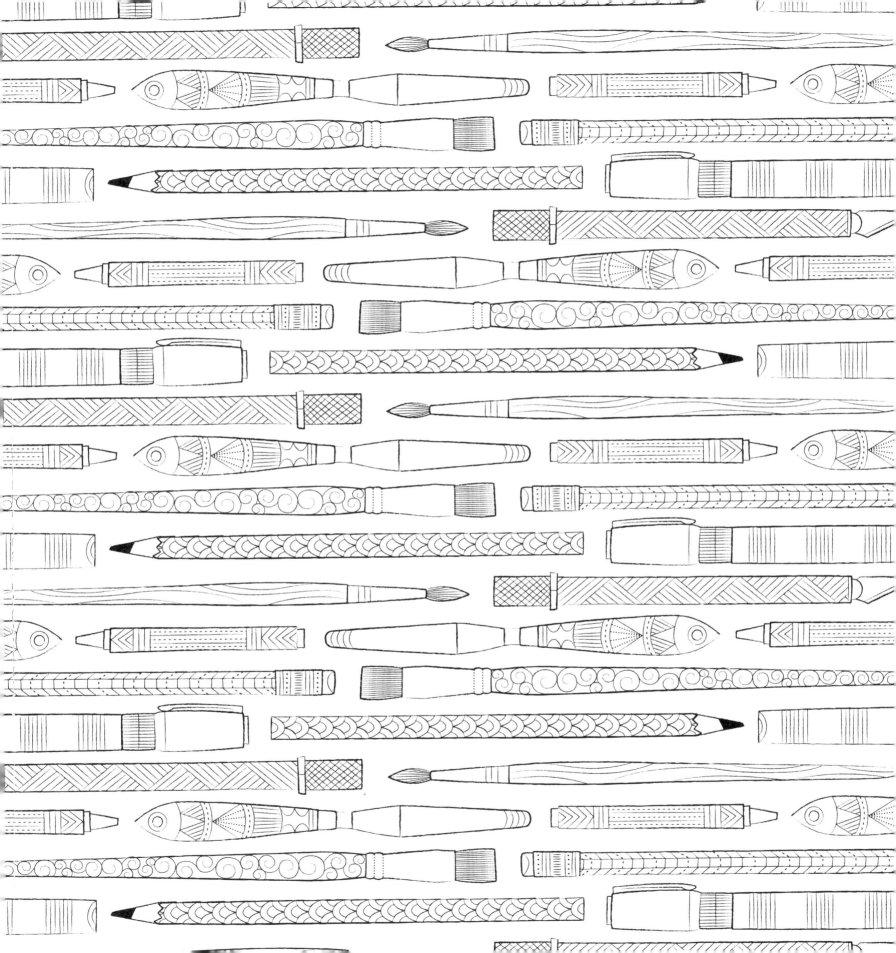

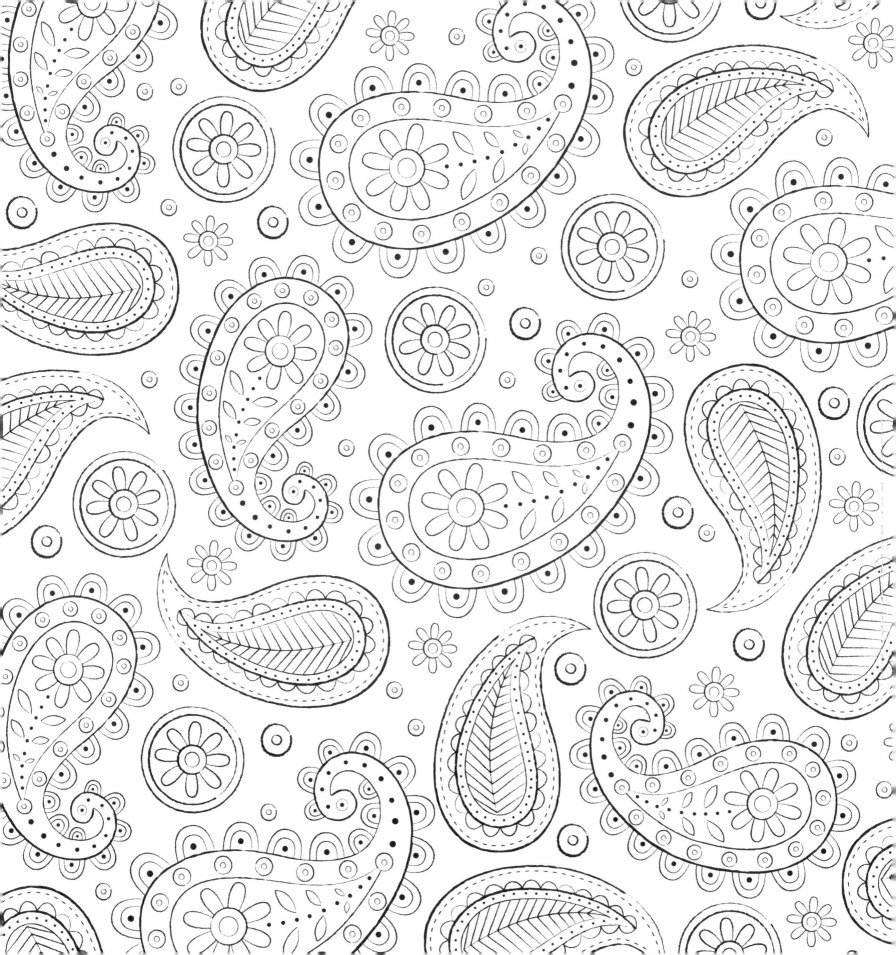

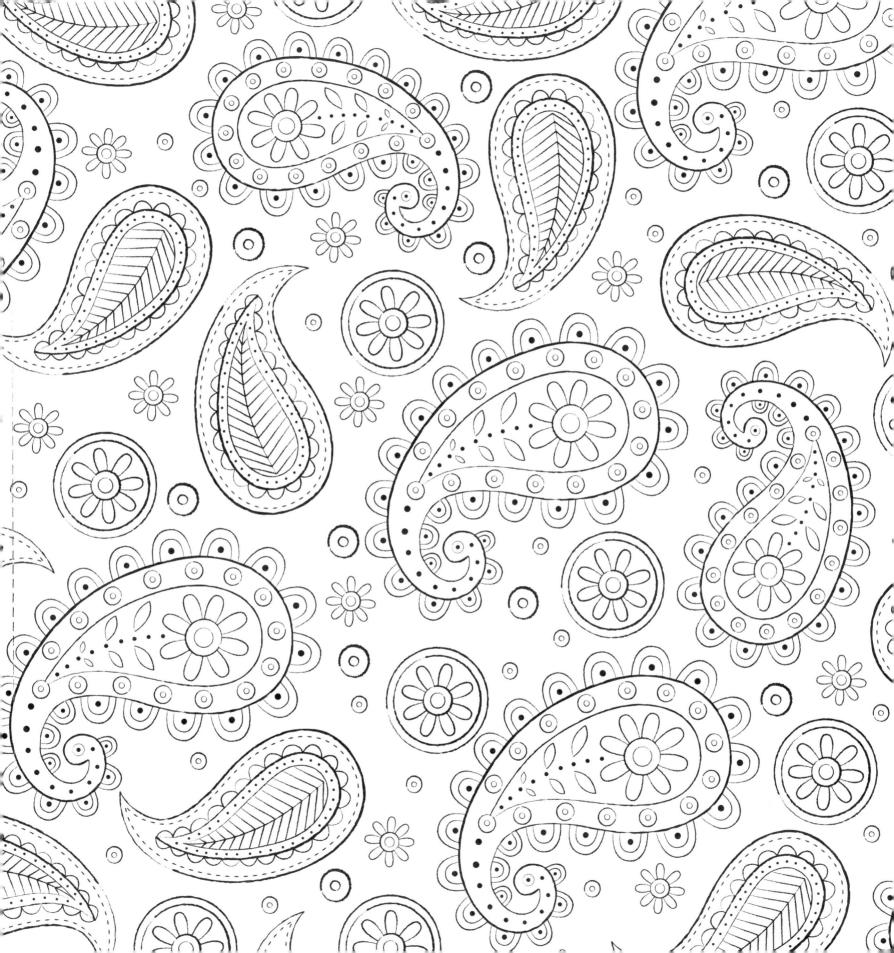

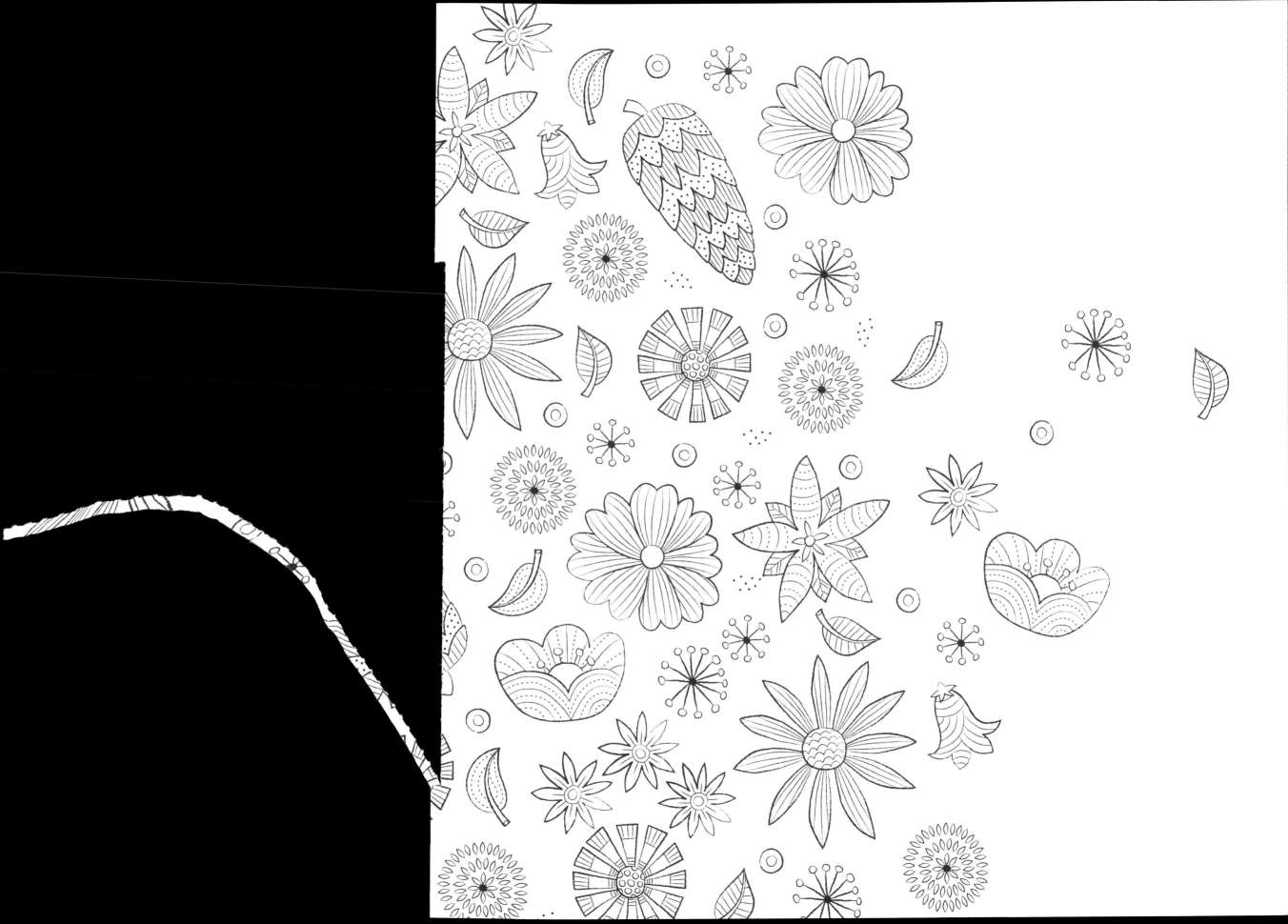

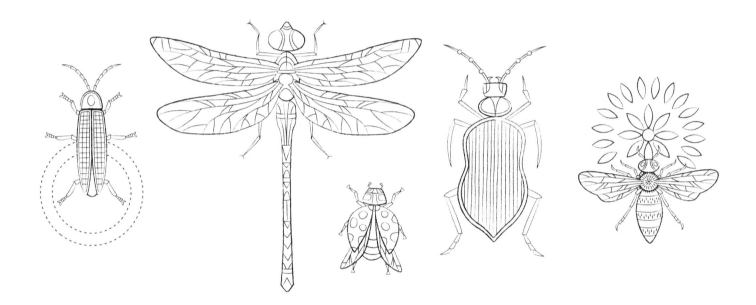

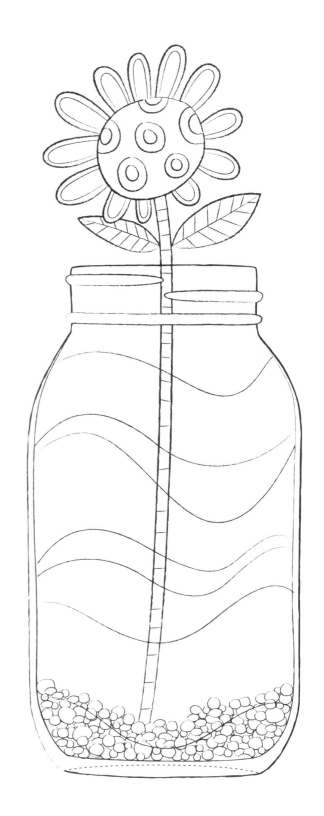

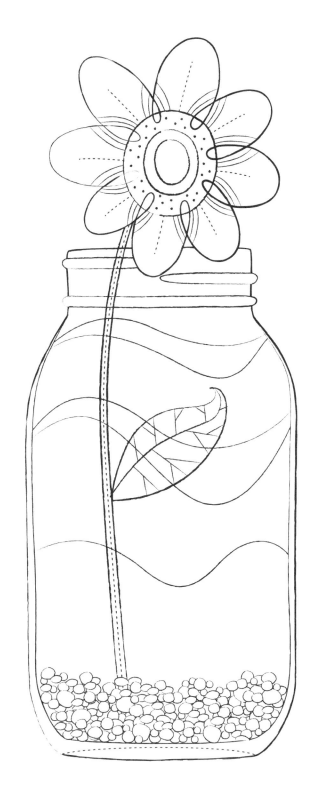